SALLY FORTH®

A WOMAN'S WORK IS NEVER DONE

by
Greg
Howard

Fawcett Columbine • **New York**

A Fawcett Columbine Book
Published by Ballantine Books

Library of Congress Catalog Card Number: 87-91866

ISBN: 0-449-90261-7

Manufactured in the United States of America

First Edition: October 1988

10 9 8 7 6 5 4 3 2 1

Women, are you plagued by the feeling that your work is never done?

Consider exploring the untapped potential of this labor-saving appliance:

7-19
howard

THIS IS SO ANNOYING. WHERE DO ALL OUR PENS GO?

I'VE LOOKED EVERYWHERE IN THIS HOUSE FOR A PEN! NOW WHAT AM I SUPPOSED TO DO?

I DROPPED ONE BEHIND THE SOFA A FEW WEEKS AGO. LET'S GO LOOK.

7-21

howard

14

18

24

WHEN I WAS LITTLE, BACK BEFORE THE HEALTH CARE INDUSTRY FELT COMPELLED TO BOMBARD US WITH DETAILS ABOUT EVERY CONCEIVABLE DISEASE, MY MOM WOULD SAY "DRINK YOUR MILK, SALLY. IT'S GOOD FOR YOU."

howard

DRINK YOUR MILK, HILARY, SO YOUR BONES DON'T GET SOFT AND CRUMBLE FROM OSTEOPOROSIS.

I THINK I LIKED MOM'S WAY BETTER.

8-23

8-29
howard

28

8-30
howard

29

9-5

howard

35

2-1

37

43

9-28
howard

47

MOM'S WORKING ON A TALK SHE HAS TO GIVE TOMORROW, HILARY, SO...

SO I MAY AS WELL START PICKING UP MY ROOM.

WHY DO YOU SAY THAT?

BECAUSE WHEN SHE HAS TO GIVE A SPEECH SHE GETS NERVOUS, AND WHEN SHE GETS NERVOUS SHE GETS GROUCHY AND WHEN SHE GETS GROUCHY SHE GOES OFF ABOUT MY MESSY ROOM.

THIS MIGHT BE A GOOD TIME TO GET A SHOVEL AND TAKE CARE OF THE DIRTY SOCKS IN FRONT OF MY CLOSET.

10-7

53

56

61

howard 11-15

62

12-2

howard

12-3

howard

Unfortunately, it isn't always possible to control how busy you are.

Sometimes staying late at the office is the only way to catch up on work.

I'VE GOT A TON OF WORK HERE, TED, SO I'M STAYING LATE. CAN YOU AND HILARY MANAGE DINNER?

First, the obligatory phone call must be made.

I DON'T KNOW, DO WHAT I DO ... YANK THE FREEZER DOOR OPEN REAL FAST, AND WHATEVER FALLS OUT YOU FIX FOR DINNER.

Next, gather all the items you need to accomplish your tasks.

Then settle down to work. The principal advantage of staying late is that you won't experience interruptions.

On the other hand, after a long day you may experience a slight drop in productivity.

12-7

howard

71

74

12-20

HAVE YOU EVER NOTICED HOW ONE PARTICULAR EMOTION GETS REAL STRONG AT CHRISTMAS?

I SURE HAVE, HONEY.

I GET VERY NOSTALGIC AT THIS TIME OF YEAR. I ESPECIALLY LIKE TO THINK BACK TO CHRISTMAS TIMES WHEN I WAS YOUR AGE.

79

12-27
howard

HER MIND RACES IN SEARCH OF A WAY TO OUTWIT THIS DIABOLICAL DEMON, BUT TIME IS RUNNING OUT.

I HAVE ABSOLUTELY NO IDEA WHAT TO GET OUT FOR DINNER.

HOW ABOUT YOUR CHECK-BOOK?

AND SO, WITH HELP FROM A DIMINUTIVE PASSERBY, OUR HEROINE STANDS ASTRIDE THE VANQUISHED VILLAIN, CHECK-BOOK IN HAND.

IF YOU'RE GOING TO TALK WEIRD LIKE THIS IN THE RES-TAURANT, MOM, I'M SITTING AT A DIFFERENT TABLE.

1-25

howard

EXPERTS SAY WOMEN CARRY THE HEAVIER BURDEN AT HOME BECAUSE MEN CONTINUE TO HARBOR A DEEP-SEATED RELUCTANCE TO DO CHORES TRADITIONALLY ASSIGNED TO WOMEN. TO BREAK THIS PATTERN IT MAY BE NECESSARY TO DESIGN APPLIANCES THAT APPEAL TO THE MASCULINE NATURE.

FOR EXAMPLE, THE FORTHS JUST BOUGHT A NEW VACUUM CLEANER.

... AND THIS IS THE TACHOMETER. IT RED LINES AT 7000 RPMS.

VERY IMPRESSIVE, TED. HAVE YOU HAD IT OUT ON THE OPEN CARPET YET?

2-21

howard

3-1
howard

YOU'D THINK THAT SOMEONE WITH ENOUGH ENERGY TO RUN FIVE MILES WOULD HAVE ENOUGH ENERGY TO PUT THE TOILET SEAT BACK DOWN.

ARE YOU STILL AWAKE, SAL? WHAT THE HECK ARE YOU DOING?

3-20
howard

THINK-ING.

IT'S 2 A.M. WHAT CAN POSSIBLY BE SO IM-PORTANT THAT IT CAN'T WAIT TILL MORNING?

THINGS LIKE WHETHER OUR MARRIAGE IS TRULY SOLID... THINGS LIKE WHETHER WE SHOULD HAVE ANOTHER CHILD... YOU CONSIDER THOSE UNIMPORT-TANT?

ME? ARE YOU KIDDING? I WAS JUST LYING HERE HOPING YOU'D WAKE ME UP TO TALK ABOUT THEM.

3-22

105

4-8 howard

5-13
howard

121

6-3